D1305837

Exotic Shorthair Cats

Stephanie Finne

Checkerboard Library

An Imprint of Abdo Publishing
www.abdopublishing.com

www.abdopublishing.com

Published by Abdo Publishing, a division of ABDO, PO Box 398166, Minneapolis, MN 55439.
Copyright © 2015 by Abdo Consulting Group, Inc. International copyrights reserved in all
countries. No part of this book may be reproduced in any form without written permission from
the publisher. Checkerboard Library™ is a trademark and logo of Abdo Publishing.

Printed in the United States of America, North Mankato, Minnesota.
032014
092014

THIS BOOK CONTAINS
RECYCLED MATERIALS

Cover Photo: Photo by Helmi Flick
Interior Photos: Getty Images pp. 18–19; Glow Images p. 5; Photos by Helmi Flick pp. 11, 15, 17, 21;
    Thinkstock pp. 1, 7, 8–9, 12–13

Series Coordinator: Bridget O'Brien
Editors: Tamara L. Britton, Megan M. Gunderson
Art Direction: Renée LaViolette

Library of Congress Cataloging-in-Publication Data

Finne, Stephanie, author.
    Exotic shorthair cats / Stephanie Finne.
        pages cm. -- (Cats. Set II)
    Audience: Ages 8-12.
    Includes index.
    ISBN 978-1-62403-324-7
    1. Exotic shorthair cat--Juvenile literature. 2. Cats--Juvenile literature. I. Title.
    SF449.E93F56 2015
    636.8'2--dc23
                                    2013046915

Contents

Lions, Tigers, and Cats

There are 37 different cat species. These include the mighty lion and the tiny house cat. All cats belong to the family **Felidae**.

About 3,500 years ago, ancient Egyptians began taming wild cats. They taught these cats to keep their stored food free of **rodents**. This relationship became so important that Egyptians came to believe cats were sacred.

Over time, other cultures began keeping **domestic** cats. Today, there are more than 40 different cat **breeds**. One of these is the beautiful and affectionate exotic shorthair cat.

The exotic shorthair will give you a hug when you pick it up!

Exotic Shorthair Cats

Exotic shorthair cats are Persian cats with shorter fur. Legends say Persian cats came from Persia in the 1600s. This area became modern-day Iran.

In the late 1950s, several American **breeders** crossed short-haired cats with Persians. The kittens had a Persian cat's features but not the Persian's long coat. The kittens had round faces, stocky frames, and **plush**, short coats.

These new kittens could not be shown with the Persian breed. But, the American shorthair breed was an open registry. So the new shorthair cats were registered there. The cats began to win high marks in the show ring.

In 1966, the **Cat Fanciers' Association (CFA)** recognized this new **breed**. At first, the cats were called sterlings because of their silver color. But soon, kittens with other coat colors were born. The CFA decided to name the breed exotic shorthairs. The cats seemed exotic because their coat colors did not exist in other shorthair cats.

Today, breeders are still trying to find a more fitting name for the exotic shorthair breed.

Qualities

Exotic shorthair cats are gentle and calm. They do not demand a lot of attention, but they love to be near people. They love to cuddle up next to their humans or on a lap.

These cats are playful. They will jump after toys for hours. But they are also independent enough to be left alone. They will be content watching dripping water or gazing outside. They do not need to be entertained.

Exotic shorthair cats make great family pets. They are very easygoing. They adjust easily when introduced to children and other pets. They will soon become playmates with all family members.

Many people believe female cats are sweeter than males. However, male exotic shorthairs are more affectionate than females. Females seem to have more important things to do than cuddle. Keep this in mind when choosing your exotic shorthair!

The exotic shorthair is known as a "teddy bear cat." This is because of its short hair and sweet face.

Coat and Color

The exotic shorthair's coat isn't like the coat of any other short-haired cat. The cat's medium-length fur is an even length on the body. It is shorter on the cat's face and legs.

The coat is also very **dense**. It is similar to the winter coat of a bear. This makes the exotic shorthair **unique**. No other **breed** has a coat like it!

The exotic shorthair is easy to groom. The short coat will not **mat** or tangle. During **shedding** time, daily combing is required. A quick brush to remove loose hair is all it needs. This makes grooming the exotic shorthair much easier than grooming their Persian cousins.

The exotic shorthair's coat can be any color. The most common are blue, black, cream, red, tortoiseshell, and **tabby**. The first exotics were silver. Today, silver is rare. No matter what color or pattern, the exotic shorthair is a charming pet.

Since it is so easy to groom, the exotic shorthair is sometimes called the lazy man's Persian cat.

Size

Exotic shorthair cats are round and heavily boned. They are cobby, or stocky, cats that are well balanced. The legs are short and thick and end in round paws.

The head of the exotic shorthair is round. It features full cheeks and a flat, snub nose. The eyes are large and round.

Exotic shorthairs look round all over. But underneath, they are solid muscle. Their padded bodies and thick fur keep these cats warm. They like to sleep in cool places. In fact, they would rather sleep on cool tiles or in the sink than in bed with their humans.

Exotic shorthairs often weigh 7 to 14 pounds (3.2 to 6.4 kg).

Care

Like all cats, your exotic shorthair will require regular checkups with a veterinarian. The cat will receive **vaccines** and an overall exam at its vet visit. The vet will also **spay** or **neuter** your cat.

Wild cats bury their waste. Your exotic shorthair will have the same instinct. Provide a **litter box** for your cat to use. Do not forget to remove waste from it every day.

Exotic shorthairs will also need to sharpen their claws. Wild cats do this on trees. **Domestic** cats need a scratching post. A scratching post will save furniture and carpets from kitty's claws! With a little love and attention, the exotic shorthair will be a fun, easy addition to your family.

An exotic shorthair's eyes will sometimes water. They will need to be wiped clean.

Feeding

Like all cats, exotic shorthairs are carnivores. They need meat as part of a healthy diet.

There are different types of cat food to choose from. Canned foods are moist. Semimoist foods are soft but do not need to be refrigerated. Dry foods are harder and help clean your cat's teeth. Choose a food that is labeled "complete and balanced." It will contain the **nutrients** your cat needs.

Along with food, be sure to always provide fresh water for your cat. It needs clean water every day. Keep food and water dishes clean by washing them often.

Your exotic shorthair may enjoy an occasional treat. But do not overfeed your cat. House cats can easily become overweight. Controlling portion sizes will help your cat stay healthy.

Cats like to eat treats.
These can help clean
a cat's teeth!

Kittens

Most cats are able to mate when they are 7 to 12 months old. However, exotic shorthair cats mature slower than other cats. They may not be ready to reproduce until they are older. After mating, female cats are **pregnant** for about 65 days. There are usually four kittens per **litter**.

The kittens are born blind, deaf, and helpless. After 10 to 12 days, they can see and hear. They also get teeth. At three weeks, they can walk and explore. Many **breeders** say that, compared to other cats, exotic shorthairs will be the first to open their eyes and climb out of their box.

For the first five weeks, kittens drink their mother's milk. Then, they are **weaned** onto solid food. The kittens continue to learn and grow during this time. They are able to leave their mother at 12 to 16 weeks old.

Exotic kittens are quiet and loving.

Buying a Kitten

Exotic shorthair cats are active but do not demand a lot of attention. They like to be near their owners. For some people, they are the perfect pet!

Have you decided the exotic shorthair is the right cat for your family? If so, look for a reputable **breeder**. Good breeders sell healthy cats. They provide **vaccinations**. They can also tell you the history of your exotic shorthair.

When you find a breeder, be sure to visit the kittens. Look for a kitten that is curious and active. Check to be sure you are not allergic to the kitten.

Before bringing home your cat, you will need to have some supplies in place. Food and water dishes, food, and a **litter box** are needed right away. You are now ready for your new friend! With regular health care, good food, and plenty of attention, your exotic shorthair will be a loving member of your family for 12 to 14 years.

A breed rescue is another place to find cats in need of a loving home.

Glossary

breed - a group of animals sharing the same ancestors and appearance. A breeder is a person who raises animals. Raising animals is often called breeding them.

Cat Fanciers' Association (CFA) - a group that sets the standards for judging all breeds of cats.

dense - thick or compact.

domestic - tame, especially relating to animals.

Felidae (FEHL-uh-dee) - the scientific Latin name for the cat family. Members of this family are called felids. They include lions, tigers, leopards, jaguars, cougars, wildcats, lynx, cheetahs, and domestic cats.

litter - all of the kittens born at one time to a mother cat.

litter box - a box filled with cat litter, which is similar to sand. Cats use litter boxes to bury their waste.

mat - to form into a tangled mass.

neuter (NOO-tuhr) - to remove a male animal's reproductive glands.

nutrient - a substance found in food and used in the body. It promotes growth, maintenance, and repair.

plush - thick and soft.

pregnant - having one or more babies growing within the body.

rodent - any of several related animals that have large front teeth for gnawing. Common rodents include mice, squirrels, and beavers.

shed - to cast off hair, feathers, skin, or other coverings or parts by a natural process.

spay - to remove a female animal's reproductive organs.

tabby - a coat pattern featuring stripes or splotches of a dark color on a lighter background. Individual hairs are banded with light and dark colors.

unique (yoo-NEEK) - being the only one of its kind.

vaccine (vak-SEEN) - a shot given to prevent illness or disease.

wean - to accustom an animal to eating food other than its mother's milk.

Websites

To learn more about Cats, visit **booklinks.abdopublishing.com**. These links are routinely monitored and updated to provide the most current information available.

Index